THE INVENTION OF HONEY

THE INVENTION OF HONEY

RICARDO STERNBERG

SIGNAL EDITIONS IS AN IMPRINT OF VEHICULE PRESS MONTREAL CANADA

ACKNOWLEDGEMENTS

Some of these poems have appeared in the following publications: *Poetry*, *The Paris Review*, *The Nation*, *Canadian Literature*, *The Canadian Forum*, *Ploughshares*, *The Virginia Quarterly*, *Antigonish Review*, *The American Poetry Review*, *West Coast Poetry Review*, *Pebble*, *Matrix*, *Green House*, *Small Moon*, *Saturday Night*. "The Angel and the Mermaid" originally published in *Small Moon* was published in *Pushcart Prize III: Best of the Small Presses, 1978-1979*. I thank Douglas Thompson, Ross Shideler and Stephen Yenser for their continued patience and assistance with these poems over many years.

Published with the assistance of The Canada Council.

Signal Editions editor: Michael Harris
Cover design: JW Stewart
Photograph of the author: Arlene Collins
Typeset in Monotype Centaur by ECW Type & Art
Printed by Les Editions Marquis Ltee

Canadian Cataloguing in Publication Data

Sternberg, Ricardo, 1948–
    The Invention of Honey

Poems.
ISBN 1-55065-006-8

I. Title

PS8587.T4711I69 1990   C811'.54   C91-090011-6
PR9199.3.S83I69 1990

Véhicule Press, P.O.B. 125, Place du Parc Station, Montreal, Quebec H2W 2M9.

Distributed in Canada by the University of Toronto Press and in the United States by University of Toronto Press (Buffalo) and Bookslinger (St. Paul, Minnesota).

Printed in Canada on acid-free paper

To my parents, Hilgard and Carolina

CONTENTS

"O Socrates, the world cannot for an instant
endure to be only what it is."

— *Paul Valéry*

ONE

THE TRUE STORY OF MY LIFE

At the age of three
I was promised in marriage
to a neighbouring princess
and took to heart
my father's interests.

As prescribed by her religion
I immediately underwent
strange rites of purification,
submitting myself to an awkward diet
of eggs laid under a waxing moon.

I was apprenticed
to seven masters
who, through a painful
pedagogical process
much in vogue in those days

though later discredited,
instructed me in the arts
of etiquette, fencing,
ballroom dancing, history,
archery, rhetoric and erotics.

She arrived from Vienna,
my dancing teacher;
a woman who despite
her advanced age and weight
glided gracefully into my life.

Beaming at me
from behind thick glasses
the Viennese was thorough
and ours was a tour
of what the world's feet
had been doing across the ages.

She was, however, prejudiced
against all modern movements:
the grotesque stomp of savages.
So what I learned and polished
were the saraband, the minuet,
the gavotte, pavane and quadrille.

But most difficult,
demanding the greatest grace,
the courtship dance:
a complicated series of gestures,
a slow, erotic posturing,
and finally the chaste embrace
of bride and groom.

One master enchanted me.
He was a one-eyed gypsy
who ingratiated himself
into my father's household
by magically removing
the unseemly wart
that blemished my sister's
happiness, my father's
designs on another kingdom.

His lessons were to provide me
with what my father called
Personal Magnetism.
I was made to meditate forever
on the cryptic remark
with which he would leave me:
self-maintenance is the smallest
duty of the human species.

With another master
I spent long hours
untangling the snarled
lineage of the girl;
but the incestuous lines
crossed so often,
their imagination for names
was so limited,
that I grew confused, lost appetite
and though severely punished
gave up that line of study
satisfied that she was indeed
the issue of man and woman.

The princess herself
I never saw, though photographs
were sent daily from the palace:
a pale, frightened girl at first
and later, the sneering beauty
astride her stallion.

She would send me perfumed notes
recounting the exploits
of her favourite pet: *Today,*
she would write of the alligator
he snapped a hummingbird
clean out of the air.

My twentieth year
was entirely devoted
to the study of a groom's
manner on the wedding night.

Instructed in the secrets
of zippers, buttons, clasps and snaps
my hands acquired the instinct
of searching always for flesh:

of unbuttoning, unzipping,
unclasping, unfastening,
bypassing at any rate
cloth that stood in the way.

At the age of twenty-one
I sent the princess
three red roses and a note that read:
Je regrette;
I robbed my father's coffers,
eloped with the middle daughter
of the pastry cook.

THREAD AND NEEDLE

Stern, starched, mustachioed,
my great-uncle spent the days
policing the stones in his garden,
the mangoes on his trees.
He spoke to me of the emperor.

Sinhazinha, my aunt, the seamstress,
purblind with cataracts at sixty-five,
would hand me the needle and ask:
child, thread this for me.

If I moved my head a certain way
Sinhá was inside the aquarium
lost among the ferns,
sewing and muttering prayers
oblivious to bright fish
threading in and out of her hair.

> *Silver needle, golden thimble*
> *I will sew your bride her dress.*

Sanctuary of boredom, that house
was a world, a system complete,
self-sufficient as the aquarium.

So who was it that interfered
introducing into the house
a device that could thread needles?

I no longer remember.
But soon after I touched it
the contraption would not work
or would not work as well
and Sinhá, suspecting
a demon in those gears,
turned her eyes towards one
lost inside the aquarium
and asks, again and again:
child, thread this for me.

THE INVENTION OF HONEY

Admit
from the start:
next to nothing
is what we know
about the bee.

Some have argued
that the sun cried:
the tears fell,
they took wings,
took heart and went to work.

Others have called this
poetry —
dismissing it
as hatched by men
with their heads
in the moon:
the bee is an ant
promoted for good behaviour,
given wings, a brighter suit
and the key to honey.

Very well.
The debate continues
and I do not know.

The bee is to me
as I must seem to her:
a complete mystery.

small engines running on honey

striped angels who fell for sweetness

stars shooting into the corolla of a petalled sun

THE ANGEL AND THE MERMAID

An angel fell
in love
with a mermaid.

A creature of no imagination,
the mermaid
rejected the possibility
such a being could exist,
and when he hovered over her,
so white against the blue,
would turn to her sisters
and ask
how is it that foam
has taken flight?

The angel grew sullen,
gained weight,
began to molt.

He was moved
further and further back
in the choir,
but still his lament
pierces the melody
bringing a dark cloud
to the eye of god.

It is, she whispered,
determined by laws
governing the attraction
of near-opposites.

Science can predict
the consequences:
the endless harangues
that are to ensue.

Love? What else is new?
A glandular enthusiasm,
the brain's hallelujahs:
worse than cancer.

SURGERY

The lover said:

look here,
your foliated heart
is a mystery, an onion
drawing tears.

Borrowing the delight
with which you remove
layers of my clothing

I will peel your heart
and go on peeling
until what remains
is artless and real.

Layer fell on layer
around our naked feet
until what remained
was the size of a bead:

my dwindled heart.

Oh lover, so excessive
in your zeal:
tell me again of angels
who danced on smaller fields.

MYTH

Wings
she grew that night
and flew
out the open window.

All night she spun
a supple net.

Moon, lovers, the trees,
the kiss and the stars:
on these she fixed
her strong thread.

Before the break of day
she stood back

aimed at the net
and with sunrise
— dead centre —
threw in her heart.

A MAN WITH SEX IN HIS HEAD

I have noticed lately
that day in, day out,
the air grows thicker with sex.

Everywhere I turn
the air seems constellated
by breasts, by buttocks,
by thighs; I see naked women
everywhere and I am afraid to breathe.

Tell me, good friend,
who are those sexual acrobats
on the high wire
between the buildings?
I have stood here
transfixed by what
goes on and on and on.

Already it has come
to where I keep my hands
in my pockets all day.
Leaving,
they are like Noah's birds
who bring me back news
I already know:
that the world is green
and full of sex.

I am worried.
Where will it all end?
Last night, looking at the sky,
Ursa Major began to move.

THE BODIES OF ANGELS

The bodies of angels
are pure
and sexless.
Where penis or vagina
should have been
God planted stars.

How delicate
the feet and hands!
Long and tapering,
lit by that strange
translucence,
the feet never meet
the resistance of stone,
a road's sullen stretch;

the hands never strain
but offer, incandescent,
— a gesture Oriental dancers
have tried for ages to emulate —
the true path.

Strangely enough, the wings
are their strongest limbs:
the muscles well concealed
under the fluff of feathers.

The sweetness in their faces
which makes them all look alike
is this strength, translated.

Mump's the one.
Braids words to a rope
he'll hang you with
on half a chance.
Drown you if he could
in sheer verbiage. Lyrical
he is by the ton.

Mump's the man.
If he guffaws in your bed
why blame him? Poet
of swamps, of brackish waters,
watch his eyes when surf breaks:
they roll to show their whites.

Mump is
and being is of some comfort.
Bruiser. Oaf of a man;
half-man, half-beast, he smells
of onions, beef, urine.
He grubs by the sink oblivious
to what and to who Mump is.

FOR NOW

Surely in some other realm,
love, our enterprise, is run
free of all these contradictions
or with all of them resolved
into contrapuntal harmony.

What we have must suffice.

Fish-bird beneath the ribs,
the heart never knows
if to sing, when to strike.

Yet asleep and back to back,
lovers dream the unsteady heart
made steadfast and love, a rose,
that blossomed and is about to,
forever.

A SMALL SPIDER

Only a spider, a small
missionary of sadness
I swallowed somehow
when I was distracted.

Laughter broke easily
her thin restraints
the delicate geometry
of the nets

but, patient architect,
she drew more lines,
reinforced the structure
until laughter ceased.

Only a small spider
who came in one day
of rain or of sunshine
one day like any other.

Tongue-tied, moans
were all I mustered:
lugubrious songs,
crippled lullabies.

Only a small sadness
on eight legs,
an implacable seamstress
with black thread

working behind my eyes,
but day by day
the day becomes
more like night.

FLAMENCO

The guitarist must be able
without leaving the stage
to hang one of the strings
from the moon.

Any moon will do
but the guitarist who snares
a full-blooded one
carries the obvious advantage.

This awakens in the wood
smooth and varnished
the sap of its tree —
and this tree

feeling itself hollow
throws out into the night
a lament as lovely
as it is piercing.

His fingers must be pure
forgetting what they know
so as to learn
a tune beyond themselves.

Only then, his *rasgueados*
will quicken blood,
his *tremolos* draw tears
from the eyes of virgins.

At the sound of his *arpeggios*
seraphim and archangels
descend on the stage
sweating profusely.

The music that is made
by the guitarist's heart
against the backside of the instrument
is contrapuntal to the other

and here it is superfluous
to speak of technique.
He must, however, be ready
and show no trace of surprise

nor falter in intensity
when his chair lifts from the stage
and floats above,
away from the astonished crowd.

FLUTE PLAYER

When I bring the flute
to my lips

when I let loose
music's happy hair,

hard-edged, the morning air
is changed
and no longer a woman,
I have become the bird
hidden in the reed.

THE ALCHEMIST

You will find
the laboratory
far simpler these days;
uncluttered.
The cauldron is gone,
the endless bubbling,
the stench, the maze
of pipes, the shelves
of exotic ingredients
that, however combined,
could not transmute
baseness into gold.
That is all done with.
Sold or given away
to whoever would have it.
The thin blue flame
went out.

But I have abandoned
more than tools.
The obstinate ideas
have been driven out
and I am now plagued
by something different
whose needs are simpler:
pen and paper and time
to apply one to the other.

There is no conjuring
but that which a pen
might drum
across the surface;
there is no incantation
but that which language
performs upon itself:
word linking with magic
word, the whole sustained
by the musculature of syntax.

Mystery is what remains
constant; mystery of magic
and of failure:
my nightmare of metal
forever dull,
replaced by this page
that remains blank
though I write upon it.

ONIONS

The opacity of onions
is deceiving.

The onion is a crystal ball
that makes you cry
for future sorrows.

I was told this
by my grandmother
tired of the daily drama
by the sink.

FRANCIS'S BARN

Laudie Waples, a neighbour, owns the barn
but with husband dead and the livestock gone
her farm is up for sale;
the barn is his for use in winter.

The whole of winter he keeps the herd inside;
each held in place by a metal yoke.

Disturbed by voices, barn swallows fly
zig-zags about the nave. *Nave?*
Shafts of light on plaster walls,
rows of stalls like narrow, private pews.

Francis tells us of lightning —
how, when it strikes the barn,
the current moves through the yokes
dropping the herd, stunned, to their knees;
and once, when he himself was struck,
how the bucket flew from his hands
and a column of milk rose in the air.

BUFFALO

I have wrestled a buffalo
into this poem
the least I could do
for an endangered species.

I have given him a tree
for shade, a stream
to slake his thirst.

A hulk of night stranded
on my gold-green pasture
he shakes stars from his fur,
paws thunder into the ground.

The reader is to blame
who brings red into the poem.

TWO

When the woman with the mapa mundi
tattooed on her behind said boys
the world is yours for the taking, I
for one, remained a skeptic. I knew

the rich got to the table first
and once done, started on seconds.
The rest wait their turn, blue
with hunger, sucking on empty spoons.

Two occupations broke my father
and I don't mean jobs. Then he fled
to the promised land, bruised
and burdened with an immigrant's heart.

He lives in America for Christ, work,
the bottle: sits on the sofa,
half plastered, Sunday mass on the tube
in a vernacular only half understood.

Once, I walked into the room and saw
the old man kneeling on the carpet.
He bowed his head to a flickering
on the screen and then keeled over.

Every month the old geezers gather
to lick wounds from skirmishes
no history book will ever register.
After a joint, sometimes I join them:

the intelligentsia of the old country
sweating in the greaseshops of Oakland
alongside blacks and chicanos
they, too quickly, learned to hate.

Before the night is done, as if on cue,
they will raise a silent toast
to Petras' letter framed on the wall.
Written just before he was neutralized

by the NKVD, it brims with cheery news
but ends in a biblical non-sequitur,
"We particularly like Psalm 102."
You might call it their drinking song:

I am like the pelican in the wilderness.
I am like an owl of the desert.
My days are like a shadow that declineth
and I am withered like grass.

I remember the morning he came
into my room; I knew something was wrong.
"Today is a sad day. Day of shame.
The Americans have published a map

no longer showing our beloved Lithuania
as disputed territory." And then he wept.
Our beloved Lithuania? It means nothing
to me except some names, photographs

and a territory staked in his memory
that stands between us and which I cannot traverse.
That drunken woman offering us her bum:
what else has history been this century?

Gin and tonic
unravels the party,
the poet and the night.
Stars blur,
grow dim and scatter
and the way home
is lost forever.

The streets become
interminable, angles
breed in the dark.
The poet drifts
and blesses himself
past the church.
Then it happens:

The closed fan
which was himself
flares open: one
preaches the evil
of excessive drinking;
the poet swears
future abstinence.

Another,
the gregarious,
addresses strangers,
vagrant dogs . . .
The poet retraces
his unsteady steps
to apologize.

The tragic one
keeps intoning:
the way home
is lost forever.
But a tear sparkles
in the poet's eyes
and he follows it home.

At his doorstep
he stumbles,
snaps shut the fan,
fumbles against
the sudden silence
and opens the door.

SONG OF A CROW, DYING

Goodbye to the sun
my father
who blessed me
obstinately every day.
I cursed not being made
in the image of your brightness.

My mother the moon
did no better.
Her love for white
silk gowns, slippers,
betrayed her rejection.

Goodbye to corn:
minaret of sweetness.
Farmers, forgive me
my daily pillage.

Forgive me also
field-mice, my brothers,
for I cackled at your fear
when my shadow loomed
large over those fields.

My little sisters
the ants:
I leave you knowing
that like Antigone
you will come out
and bury your brother.

That you do so in self-interest
will not diminish my gratitude.

Who is to know
if Erasmus, alone,
brewing his tea,
for once considers
the steps taken
that brought him
pell-mell and wide-
eyed to where he is.

Who is to know
if he — still alone —
begins subtracting
the years and steps
until standing again
at the blind hour
of some choice.

Who I am today —
this bearded man
brewing his tea
alone alone alone
can be blamed on
the man I was then
and the poor devil
knew of no choice.

Travelled backwards,
the road reveals
its hidden fork;
a retroactive wound
flares briefly
at the disclosure.

The kettle whistles
and Erasmus, alone,
turns to other matters.

When I gave her smiles
she gave me a wooden bell.
I have never known such sorrow.

When I gave her some tears
she gave me a small drum.
Now the neighbours know my joy.

When I gave her silence,
the green bird she gave me
flew down my throat.

It is with his voice
and none other
that now I sing in sleep.

TIA

Of this one I now speak
but soft and low
for I do not wish
to disturb her sleep.

Were my words to reach her
on that other shore
she would be embarrassed
to hold even this small
a stage. Her role
had been to always play
second to married sisters.

A fragile thing, she was
myopic, rheumatic, prone
to spells of dizziness.
Once, under the mango tree
that shadowed the entire house
she began to fall but reached
for a trailing vine,
regained her balance
and from behind thick glasses
smiled at me: Tarzan,
she said, and shuffled away.

A believer in icons
and in appeasing heaven
with prayer and promise,
she kept the household altar
outside her bedroom door:
A large niche painted blue,
speckled with golden stars.

Her patron was St. Francis:
A bird to each shoulder,
the wolf curled at his feet.

Paulo, her brother-in-law,
a feisty bantam, an atheist,
in arguments would threaten
to make out of that niche,
a cage for his macaw.

In retrospect, I understand
those were rituals
enacted since before I was born,
meant to alleviate boredom,
understood, I think, as such.

As when, soaked in cheap cologne,
Tia drifted through the house
on a cloud of rose or jasmine:

upstairs rushed her sister
then down some minutes later,
a moist hanky to her nose
to sit frozen in a sulk.

But these were exceptions.

Shuttered against the heat,
the house droned and they slept.

When I left for the States
at fifteen, she whispered
she would be gone
long before my return. And was.
But in my dreams she knits
a dream that has no end:

in a perfumed forest,
a parrot squawking on his shoulder,
Tarzan bows to St. Francis,
swings from a vine,
and steps to her back porch.

Those darker moments I keep
in this Chinese puzzle box:
to the soft blue lake
inlaid on the lid
the fern shoots bend as if by wind.

It takes forty-seven
different steps to open:
a complicated sequence
I half-remember,
half-wish to forget.

And every time I open it
they are still there
crawling like ants:
my dearest,
my darkest seconds.

THE WEAVER

It was time, I think, that wove
our lives together: the shuttle
of conversation moved between us
easily before we fell asleep.

Years ago I sensed a pattern
emerging between the selvedges.
Not perfect, mind you, but *there*:
the bad times kept to the background

by the bold arabesque of our flair —
the shape of our shared experience
(if you will forgive me the jargon).
Memory held that design in place?

Perhaps. But I look at him today
and cannot, for the life of me,
remember what held us together,
tell you what drives us apart,

or who's breaking whose heart.

THE MYTH OF LOVERS

From the timbers
of a sudden kiss
they built a tower
and then ensconced
themselves within.

So high it was
at night the stars
were hieroglyphics
in the window's blackboard,
while each morning
the beast of light
would rise to set
the slate on fire.

They told the myths
of lovers everywhere
then became adept
at silence and gymnastics,
forsaking words
for the body's braille.

So who broke one day
the silence and the spell
to bring that tower down?

They found themselves again
on level ground: pedestrians
waiting for what was late
or would not arrive.

AWAKENED BY THE PHONE, 3 A.M.

I have been told of fish
reeled from the dark
by electric gear so quickly
they break the surface
already dead, eyes blasted,
my heart a small disaster.

FROM A LINE OF DARIO

"da al viento la cabellera"

With no dissenting votes
we gave to the wind her hair.
It brushes your cheeks,
now it brushes mine.

To the bee and to
the hummingbird:
her breasts.
We envy them the sweetness
that will be gathered there.

To the ocean belong
both her feet.
They will become
two inseparable
incredible fish
who may come out to leave
strange prints
beckoning bachelors
to walk into the sea.

We give the ocean
both her feet
and we warn you.

Many claimed her hands:
A tree wanted them
for fruit that would
be eager, for fruit
that would not wait.

A flock of birds
petitioned for her hands
claiming poetic justice
would be served were
   the feet in the water
to be echoed by
   the hands in the air.

We agree with this logic;
give instead to the tree
her ears
that it may hear itself
stretch and grow.

Whether orioles
fly these skies
I do not know.

Enough to say
that birds attend:
a generic presence
that signals
winter is still at bay.

But oriole, the word,
flutters around me now
as it has all week
unaddressed
until at last I write

south

and it goes.

ERASMUS CHALLENGED BY SPRING

His tropical glands
secrete the stuff,
his insides churning:
come spring, he wants
to be like trees
so arms extended
he welcomes the birds.

A rank mango for a heart
this lyricism
does not get him far.
The birds read trouble
in his moist eyes
ignore the nests
erected at the elbows
and fly to simpler trees.

After the third day he desists.
Humbled and in a sulk
he writes:
surely it is to rebuke us
that the world flares again
when winter within us
settles as the only season.

Your charge vacillates —
founders, in fact,
in this dizzying tide.

On every question he is
of two minds and wrong,
usually, on both counts.

His heart is perplexed.
To whom does it owe allegiance
if not to itself?

But what *doesn't* it want?

Cuff him in the head
as you did with Saul,
strike him in his Volvo

blind and illuminated.
In our relative kingdom
grant him, for once,

the fulcrum of a single
irrefutable belief.
Then sit back in heaven

and watch him go.

Il Miglior Fabbro,
I am humbled, indeed
almost paralysed
by Your ingenuity,
Your craftsmanship.

Elephant, tapir,
crocodile, mongoose,
ant, lizard, fly...
I have omitted much
but need not continue
as my point is made:
lightning strikes You
time and again.

Your every hit a home run?

Man is sometimes
less than wonderful.
Perhaps you hesitated
as we forever seem to.
But I may be wrong
and we may yet surprise
ourselves. Two weeks ago

I planted seeds
brought back from Brazil
last summer. According
to Your designs, they begin
to display some green.

I did not know the seeds
would be raised in the air
by the push of sprouts
then serve as a sheath
for the curled, new leaf.
I have no words
to express my amazement
at Your economy of means.

Brought from the tropics
then in obedience
to a sweet injunction,
the closed fist of a seed
unfurls a green banner
among the cacti on a sill
above my snowbound yard.

Perhaps we too can surge,
sprout green wings though
I mean this metaphorically.
(Indeed what I ask for
is feet rooted to the ground).
Perhaps we will learn in time
to trust the script, in time
to abide by Your metaphors.

THREE

DOUBLE ROOT

Two feet
and out of two feet grow
two legs and
of two legs a man is made
confused by his double root.

The left: an old aunt
chaste and proper
like a nun;
the right: this rake
with thin moustache
dreaming of convertibles
and Italian suits.

Since the right
decided it had enough
and in a contrite mood
began to walk toward church,
since the left
seemed to acquiesce,
it is a dark mystery
that I am here
among the *putas* again.

RE-INVENTING THE WHEEL

It was no gentle thing
the love that rolled me
as I stood perplexed
at the gates of winter.

Like some giant bird
that held me in its claws,
it shook the daylights
out of me and said look

look look, pointing nowhere.
My love for that woman
broke the gauges to leave
wide open the heart's valves:

The flood that rushed in!
You might say I was
in love with love itself
and who needs the aggravation.

That whole winter
a flock of crows followed me,
dark notes alighting
on the staves of trees.

At night they roosted
by the warm chimney
holding a gloomy vigil
over my restless sleep.

Here the reader ponders:
is the poet being coy?
So one sided! Surely
a *few* moments of joy?

We re-invented the wheel.
Every pleasure was blessed
as we repeated movements
ancient and entirely new.

Her hands were small sharks
skimming the salt of my skin,
my eyes, explorers lost
in her sweet geography.

We were surf, waves, breakers
in the blue sheets of that bed
while on the beach, the crows
faced our turbulence and frowned.

CROOKED SONNETS

I

Just when I thought
it was dead or dying
love like Lazarus
came back: summer,

the year I turned forty.
Once again it caught me
rolled me under its wave
threw me breathless to the beach

spitting sand and words.
What does the heart ever learn
that it did not know at fifteen?

Incongruous discipline,
a sweet short-circuit,
an unlearning is what love is.

I I

Oh what a ball
once again to be
on the edge
of love and all

that jazz I said
goodbye to years ago
when all it got me
was not enough

and then way more
than I could handle.
With what impatience

lady, I wait to return
to the floor again,
to be by you set spinning.

III

Something akin to a sweet
energy traffics between us.
Have you not noticed it, lady?
I hear an erotic whisper

behind our words, desire
in convoluted arabesques:
reined in, raring to go.
Who knows if it's love, the flame

we hide and want to reveal?
Twinned power plants, our hearts
feed off each other and,

since love is distributive,
send the excess humming
to the grid around us.

IV

Your ups and downs, hesitations,
twists, turns, intricate manoeuvres
have, for the time being,
exhausted your dedicated lover.

She's had it with you, pal,
to put it mildly.
She's probably decked up some doll
to look like you and is this very moment

pushing long needles, barbecue spits
deep into its little heart.
Can acupuncture fix a heart that is broken?

Time can — or so sang the Righteous Brothers
back when I believed the simple pleasures were
and love was the brain going to sleep.

SNOW WHITE'S STEP-MOM

Rouge, lipstick, mascara,
the creams and emollients
pushed on her by quacks
help but not enough

to allow her to forget
angles, apertures, light.
A court photographer
learns to fudge the focus.

What time has not undone
is the power of those eyes
that dare him to notice
what the mirror tells her

just before it shatters.

She writes that she has not been well
and adds "but this will not be news."
She complains of the rise in the cost of living
and notes that Alfredo, the parrot, has died.
"Or feigns to have." She is not sure except
the bird has not stirred in a fortnight.
"Do parrots hibernate?" and for all I know
Alfredo, who claimed kinship to Caruso, does.
"I am a woman who has chosen to live
in order to spite my final suitor."
We both know that booze sidetracked Ulysses
and how, drunk herself, she splintered the loom.
"The day after I exhale my last breath
let me be consumed by flames. Then forgotten."

Nightingales fallen from grace
singing from amongst the reeds
the stars, your inamoratas,
will not be croaked down
and you cannot leap that far.

What do you offer?
A balloon of ambition
and two eyes
that look at the world
moist with desire.

Grown oversentimental
you think you can woo the world
with your lugubrious melodies,
your antics on the darkened lawn.
Quick to jump

at flattering conclusions
you forget the world's owl:
literal, winged, hungry,
poised above you
then swooping,

fat frogs.

THE EGOIST

That little bureaucrat, the heart,
has numbers up its sleeves;
tucked between the songs,
it keeps the score.

It really isn't lyrical.
Between systole and diastole
it whispers but one word:
me me me. Love?
A polished mirror for the self.

Mump's in a funk.
His girl is gone,
he drinks too much.

Drown in self-pity?
Worse: drunk, he'll
drown in the tub.

He's tried everything
but nothing works.
Now he's on his knees

begging a patron saint
to erase her image
from his mind's eye.

But it's not to be.
Sunk to his eyebrows
in the salt of grief,

Mump's in a funk
and won't pull free
for a year or two.

One among us knows
the bliss of dirt.

One among us knows
the joy of bulk.

Unfairly rebuked
by visionaries
for lacking vision,
the pig I lassoed
knows it's useless
to poetise the moon:
a bone picked clean
by starving angels.

A saint who trots
at ease with flesh,
his eyes scan
like empty plates.
He opens his mouth
and takes a bite
of his, of our
disappearing earth.

THE MAN WHO WOULD BE STATUE
ENTICES PIGEONS TO HIS SHOULDERS

Cast in my final flourish
I renounce the kingdom of gestures,
the busy kingdom of words.

I would now be still,
mute and immutable
under the dwindling stars.

Let another dawn arrive
with the stained fingers
of the all-night smoker.

I am through with questions.

Let clouds gather over this park;
rain. I remain
oblivious and dry:

a man at last free
from his own small weathers.

SCARECROW

Years I have stood
dressed in rags
while around me grew
the congregation of corn.

I was not jealous.

I blessed them while they were growing.
I blessed the field when they were gone.

My straw heart is almost gone.
The wind moves through it
with the hands of a ghost
on an empty loom.
It pleased me when sparrows
would pluck the heartstuff
and build their nests from it.
I felt then as if I flew.
But they have kept away.

I have wished for love
from the farmer's wife.
In my dreams she would come
to take from the threadbare heart
one more straw
and chew slowly on its sweetness,
looking out from the darkened field,
flying from far away into herself.
She too has kept away.

I will not be here
next year to bless the corn.

ANA-LOUCA

Antic-prone and crazy
breast-feeding her dolls
through the streets
or on Sundays marooned
by herself in a pew,
she offered her litany
of curses and profanities
to no one in particular.

Thursdays she would come
demanding that which habit
had made hers by right:
the warmed leftovers
she wolfed down, standing
against the green backdoor.
Finished, she rattled thanks
from the gates and was gone.

A packing crate her bedroom,
she slept by the docks.
Amid rags and broken dolls,
asleep and for once, quiet,
a grizzled girl
lulled by the ocean's rhythm
as if cradled in its blue arm.

PEDDLER

He appeared each spring
to clap at our gate,
the man of foreign accent,
hauling a heavy suitcase.

When the women and children
of the household gathered,
he opened it with a flourish
then clearing his throat,
chanted the merchandise:

French perfume, from Paris!
In the palm of his hand
a vial the shape of a heart.
*The exact same brand
used to advantage by Bardot!*
A whiff glazes his eyes,
he stares hard at the maid.

A llama lighter from Peru!
He snaps the tail and a blue
flame hovers above the ears.
A lobster music-box!
A photo of Prince Gillete!

Scarves, belts and brooches,
ribbons and tiny missals,
lace, soap, ointments
and once, the tail of a marmoset.

The suitcase had no bottom
or none that I ever saw
for with a shrug of his shoulders
and suddenly sullen
he shut in the best
the world had to offer.

He locked the suitcase slowly,
giving the hesitant
time for second thoughts

then bid us a brusque goodbye
and moved his magic
to the house on our left.

GUARATIBA

This is what it's like
to sleep by the rumbled

syntax of the sea:
the demagogue pours

sounds into your ears
that state nothing

but so loudly affirm:
the stretch and swell

of a sentence rising
that finally breaks

leaving in its wake
the immediate rise

of this next one:
speak in metaphors

though you miss the point:
the sea hammer strikes

and strikes again
until you agree

this harangue will not
brook your objections:

by that roar seduced,
spellbound you fall

asleep: a blue pulse
in the pillowed ear.

THE SNAIL

Where is the snail going
and why the hurry?
Who is to follow
this silver trail
he dispenses
like a man
whose purse is broken?

I take it
the snail is a minister
without portfolio
officiating difficult disputes
between temperamental flowers:
explaining to the rose
that the geranium too
has a right to shine.

I take it
the snail is a garden impresario
convincing the marigold bud
that the time is ripe and
shyness apart, she must come out;
urging all flowers to do their best
then congratulating himself
backstage
on a successful show.

If he is seen at night
perfectly still
at the end of his shining trail,
if only his sensitive antlers
move,
the snail is dreaming
of some day
plying his trade
between the stars.

NO WONDER THE WOOD

Sacrificed, nailed into a shape
that held dull, exhausted clothes,
no wonder the wood
moans like a stricken beast
in a dark corner of the room.

It is a yearning for foliage,
fantasy, the arabesque of branch.
Rococo legs that want to sink,
dig deep and become roots
while every drawer whispers
of the absence of birds.

Coffee rings rise, the ghosts of fruit;
the cigarette burn is a charred season.

Tomorrow it will be outside.
Next to the horse-chestnut,
with legs deep in mulch,
with drawers emptied and opened,
there to persuade the birds —

to wrest green from planed wood.

If a horse is standing
perforce it is somewhere.

It is a green prairie
he stands on
with no circumscribing
fence — imagine green
that goes on forever.

He stands solitary
sunk into his sense
of being a horse
alone in the shade.

The poem has grown:
green prairie and a horse
the sun and something else
that provides that shade.

It is the apple-tree;
fruitless, the foliage
shaped like a bell
and here, yes, a fence,
hexagonal and white
protects its space.

A bird flies out.

You said the horse...
Yes. Stood in the shade.
One side of the hexagon
has two rails broken
so that (in a time before the poem)
the horse stepped gracefully
out of the sun, into the cool
green shade and stood still.

Now he flicks his tail
and the poem grows again:
a fly landed on his flank
and has been shooed away
into the green that goes
on outside the poem.

And here the poem ends
meeting all exigencies
save two, which are these:
to note the breeze moving
the grass into green waves
and, at the edge of the green
that is inside the poem,
on the outside of that edge,
one who stood and wrote it down.